TRICERATOPS

Written and Illustrated by
Michael W. Skrepnick

MIGHTY THREE-HORNED DINOSAUR

Enslow Elementary, an imprint of Enslow Publishers, Inc.

Enslow Elementary® is a registered trademark of Enslow Publishers, Inc.

Library of Congress Cataloging-in-Publication Data

Skrepnick, Michael William.
    Triceratops—mighty three-horned dinosaur / Michael W. Skrepnick.
        p. cm. — (I like dinosaurs!)
    Includes bibliographical references and index.
    ISBN 0-7660-2620-5
    1. Triceratops—Juvenile literature. I. Title.
    QE862.O65S57 2005
    567.915'8—dc22

                                    2004015719

Printed in the United States of America

10 9 8 7 6 5 4 3 2

Series Literacy Consultant:

Allan A. De Fina, Ph.D.
Past President of the New Jersey Reading Association
Professor, Department of Literacy Education
New Jersey City University

Science Consultant:

Philip J. Currie, Ph.D.
Curator of Dinosaur Research
Royal Tyrrell Museum
Alberta, Canada

To Our Readers: We have done our best to make sure all Internet Addresses in this book were active and appropriate when we went to press. However, the author and the publisher have no control over and assume no liability for the material available on those Internet sites or on other Web sites they may link to. Any comments or suggestions can be sent by e-mail to comments@enslow.com or to the address on the back cover.

Illustration Credits: Michael W. Skrepnick

Photo Credits: American Museum of Natural History, p. 4 (top); © Corel Corporation, p. 4 (herd); Michael W. Skrepnick, p. 14; Royal Tyrrell Museum/Alberta Community Development, p. 15.

Enslow Elementary
an imprint of
Enslow Publishers, Inc.
40 Industrial Road   PO Box 38
Box 398   Aldershot
Berkeley Heights, NJ 07922   Hants GU12 6BP
USA   UK
http://www.enslow.com

CONTENTS

WORDS TO KNOW

 **fossils (FAH suhlz)**—Bones, skin, and footprints of dead animals that have been buried for a very long time.

 **frill**—A flat plate of bone growing from the back of the head.

 **herd**—A large group of animals that travel together.

 **museum (myoo ZEE uhm)**—A building where special things are stored, studied, and shown to other people.

MEET MIGHTY TRICERATOPS

Triceratops (try SAIR uh tops) means "three-horned face" because it has three long, sharp horns.

HORNS AND TEETH

Triceratops had a horn over each eye. A smaller horn grew on its nose.

A huge, bony frill on its head made *Triceratops* look very big and mean.

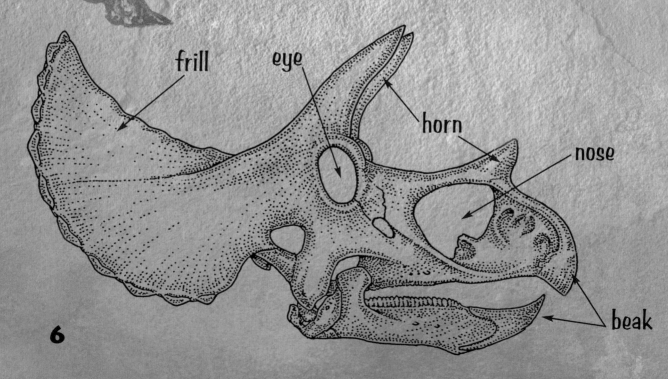

frill

eye

horn

nose

beak

Triceratops' teeth cut plants apart like scissors. The teeth wore down as they sliced and crushed plants.

New teeth pushed out the old teeth.

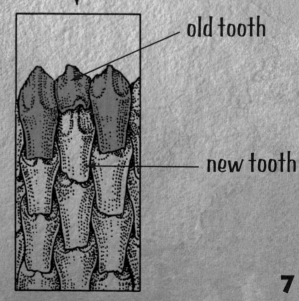

old tooth

new tooth

FOOD

Triceratops ate plants—lots and lots of plants! Sometimes it traveled many miles looking to fill its belly.

Triceratops needed a lot of food to become big and strong. It was not afraid of most other dinosaurs. But there was one dinosaur, more terrible than the rest.

ENEMIES

Here comes *T. rex!*
Triceratops was not fast enough
to outrun the huge meat eater.
It had to fight to escape *T. rex*'s
hungry jaws.

Were its long, pointed horns enough to save *Triceratops*? Sometimes *Triceratops* won the battle by badly hurting or killing *T. rex*.

TRICERATOPS BONES

Sometimes *T. rex* was the winner. It stuffed its belly with meat. Only *Triceratops'* bones were left behind.

Over millions of years, these bones turned into fossils . . . for us to find one day!

LOOKING FOR FOSSILS

Scientists search for dinosaur fossils and then dig them up. They carefully clean the fossils and move them to museums for study.

People who visit
the museums can
see these fossils.

Triceratops fossil

ANOTHER HORNED DINOSAUR

Triceratops was only one kind of horned dinosaur. Another kind was *Centrosaurus* (SEN troh SOR us). It had a long nose horn and little horns above each eye.

There is one place where scientists have found thousands of *Centrosaurus* fossil bones. The bones were all mixed up and jumbled together. How did they get there?

CENTROSAURUS HERDS

Scientists think that *Centrosaurus* traveled in large herds. After rain storms, these herds sometimes had to cross flooding rivers.

The huge herd of dinosaurs crowded into the water. Many of them drowned. Today, their fossils are found where the river buried them.

MORE HORNED DINOSAURS

There were many other kinds of horned dinosaurs. They all lived at different times. They each had horns and frills, but each dinosaur looked different from the others.

Einiosaurus
(EYE nee oh SOR us)

Chasmosaurus
(chahs moh SOR us)

Anchiceratops
(ang kee SAIR uh tops)

Styracosaurus
(sty RAH coh SOR us)

This tells scientists that these animals changed over millions of years. We call these years the Age of Dinosaurs.

Achelousaurus
(ah KEE loo SOR us)

TRICERATOPS FACTS

 Triceratops had one of the largest heads of any animal known.

 Triceratops' frill might have changed color when it got angry.

 Triceratops lived only in North America along with *T. rex*.

 Triceratops means "three-horned face."

 Triceratops did not chew its food like other plant eaters. It sliced and crushed plants in its mouth.

 Triceratops' jaws had rows of teeth growing on top of each other.

LEARN MORE

BOOKS

Dodson, Peter. *An Alphabet of Dinosaurs*. New York: Scholastic Inc., 1995.

Lessem, Don. *Scholastic Dinosaurs A to Z: The Ultimate Dinosaur Encyclopedia*. New York: Scholastic, Inc., 2003.

Thomson, Ruth. *Dinosaur's Day*. London: DK Publishing, Inc., 2000.

Williams, Judith. *Discovering Dinosaurs with a Fossil Hunter*. Berkeley Heights, N.J.: Enslow Publishers, Inc., 2004.

WEB SITES

The Children's Museum of Indianapolis
   <http://www.childrensmuseum.org/kinetosaur/
      index.html>

Discovery Kids
   <http://dsc.discovery.com/convergence/
      dinos/dinos.html>

National Geographic Kids
   <http://www.nationalgeographic.com/ngkids/
      0005/dino/>

INDEX

About the Author

Michael W. Skrepnick is an award-winning dinosaur artist. His artwork is featured in many natural history museums and appears in scientific journals, books, and magazines. Michael lives and works in Alberta, Canada, close to some of the richest deposits of late Cretaceous dinosaur fossils in the world.

Note to Parents and Teachers: The I LIKE DINOSAURS! series supports the National Science Education Standards for K–4 science. The Words to Know section introduces subject-specific vocabulary words, including pronunciation and definitions. Early readers may need help with these new words.